W9-BCN-972

PRONGHORNS

Published by Smart Apple Media
1980 Lookout Drive, North Mankato, MN 56003

Design and Production by The Design Lab/Kathy Petelinsek

Photographs by KAC Productions (Larry Ditto), Joe McDonald, Mary Ann McDonald,
Tom Stack & Associates (Erwin & Peggy Bauer, W. Perry Conway, Jeff Foott, Sharon Gerig,
Joe McDonald, Brian Parker, John Shaw, Diana Stratton)

Library of Congress Cataloging-in-Publication Data
Frisch, Aaron.
Pronghorns / by Aaron Frisch.
p. cm – (Northern trek)
ISBN 1-58340-054-0
1. Pronghorn antelope–Juvenile literature. [1. Pronghorn antelope. 2. Antelopes.] I. Title. II. Series

QL737.U52 F755   2001
599.63'9–dc21   00-050490

First Edition

2 4 6 8 9 7 5 3 1

NORTHERN TREK

PRONGHORNS

WRITTEN BY AARON FRISCH

SMART APPLE MEDIA

The American pronghorn is a peculiar creature. It can run faster than a speeding car and spot a coyote three miles (4.8 km) away. It refuses to jump over fences even though it could easily do so, and it is afraid of tall grass. With its unusual coat pattern, forked horns, and wiry legs, it looks more like a native of the African savannas than of North America's Great Plains. Yet the pronghorn has no living relative anywhere in the world, making it a most unique and fascinating animal.

MALE PRONGHORNS

(*Antilocapra americana*), called bucks, typically stand three feet (90 cm) tall at the shoulder and weigh about 120 pounds (55 kg). Females, called does, are just slightly smaller. Both sexes have long heads, small muzzles, and large pointed ears.

The pronghorn's most striking feature is its unusual forked horns. The tips of a buck's horns curl back, and one prong—the source of the animal's name—grows forward from the middle of each horn. The horns of most full-grown bucks reach 12 to 16 inches (30–41 cm) in length. Some females grow horns that are too small to have prongs or curled tips, and others grow no horns at all.

The pronghorn is built for speed. It is the second-fastest land animal on Earth. Only the cheetah is faster, and only for the first quarter-mile (402 m) or so. All of the powerful muscles that move the pronghorn's thin legs are located not in the legs themselves but in the animal's

Pronghorns are affected by few diseases, perhaps because they move often and are thinly spread across their range.

thick body. The muscles are attached to the legs by long, strong **tendons**. Because the pronghorn's legs and hooves weigh so little, they can move with blinding speed.

When pronghorns run at high speeds, their muscles burn oxygen at a very fast rate. To take in enough oxygen, pronghorns hold their mouths wide open as they run, inhaling air through wide windpipes and into huge lungs. Meanwhile, their unusually large hearts pump blood rich in **hemoglobin** to their muscles.

A pronghorn can easily maintain a speed of 45 miles (72 km) per hour for four miles (6.4 km)

To escape persistent predators or to reach distant feeding ranges, pronghorn herds can cruise along at about 30 miles (48 km) per hour for more than 10 miles (16 km).

Although pronghorns are commonly called pronghorn antelopes, they are not truly antelopes. No antelope species exist in the Americas.

or more. When running on hard ground, a sprinting pronghorn can hit speeds of close to 65 miles (105 km) per hour, although only in short bursts. Pronghorns are playful animals and often seem to run for fun. They have even been known to race moving vehicles.

In addition to its speed, the pronghorn is known for its incredible vision. Pronghorns have huge eyeballs and can spot the slightest movement—even something as small as a swaying

The heart and lungs of pronghorns are nearly four times as large as those of goats of a similar size.

When pronghorn mothers with two fawns feed, they protect the fawns by hiding them in the grass about 100 yards (91 m) apart.

shrub—several miles away. To match the power of the pronghorn's vision, a human would need to look through seven-power binoculars.

During the summer, pronghorn bucks usually travel alone, while the does gather together in small herds. In September, the bucks begin fighting to establish territories and claim mating rights. A dominant buck claiming a particularly good territory may gather a **harem** of up to 15 does. Does are pregnant for about eight months before giving birth to one or two fawns late in the spring.

A newborn fawn weighs four to nine pounds (1.8-4 kg) and takes its first steps within 30 minutes. By its third day, a pronghorn fawn can outrun a human over short distances, and by the time the fawn is three weeks old, it's faster than most **predators**. Pronghorns reach adult size in 6 months and can live up to 15 years.

Pronghorns live in open areas that offer a good view of the surrounding landscape. These include grasslands, rocky deserts, and the foothills of the Rocky Mountains. They tend to avoid large rocks, bushes, and tall grass—anything that could hide a predator.

Throughout the year, pronghorns move back and forth among several feeding ranges, eating a wide variety of plants and grasses. For most of the year, they eat tender grass shoots, small shrubs,

Pronghorns rarely reproduce in zoos and normally live no longer than one year in captivity.

and cacti. When heavy snow falls in the winter, they eat mostly **sagebrush**, which is not as nutritious as the plants they favor but is easier to find.

Healthy adult pronghorns can easily outrun wolves, mountain lions, and coyotes. Young fawns and old or crippled adults, however, are sometimes killed by these predators. When pronghorns spot an enemy, they raise the hair on their rumps to form a bright white signal to alert all other pronghorns within sight.

But pronghorns often put themselves at risk with their strange behavior. Although they can jump as far as 27 feet (8.2 m) while running, they will not hurdle even a short fence. Pronghorns have

Pronghorns' teeth never stop growing. They are constantly worn down by chewing a wide variety of plants.

been known to starve in the winter when a rancher's fence stands between them and feeding areas. Pronghorns also sometimes put themselves in danger with their curiosity. Early settlers learned that they could often lure the animals within firing range by simply waving a cloth in the air.

In 1868 and 1869, thousands of pronghorns were killed and shipped to cities in Colorado and Wyoming, where people could buy the meat of three or four animals for as little as 25 cents.

Pronghorns **evolved** in the central part of North America about 20 million years ago. At one point, 40 million of them were spread across the continent's plains, making them nearly as numerous as their large neighbors, the bison.

Pronghorns faced a truly dangerous predator for the first time when the United States government encouraged people to move to the western frontier in the 1800s. These settlers brought sheep and cattle with them. Because many settlers thought the pronghorns and bison competed for the wild grass their livestock ate, the wild animals were slaughtered in great numbers. By the end of this age of extermination, the pronghorn population had been reduced to fewer than 16,000 animals.

Finally, in the early 1900s, a widespread

conservation effort began. Laws were created to limit the number of pronghorns that hunters could kill. In some regions, pronghorns were captured alive and transported to areas where they had previously been wiped out. These conservation methods have helped. Today, nearly one million pronghorns roam across the western United States and lower parts of Canada. People traveling through this region are likely to see many pronghorns grazing on the horizon.

Pronghorns are both intelligent and observant. They are usually aware of all other animals within two or three miles (3.2 or 4.8 km).

BECAUSE THEY LIVE

on the open plains and are widely distributed, pronghorns are commonly seen in the wild. They are easy to spot from a distance but will run off if humans come too close. To get a better look, use binoculars. You can often see pronghorns along the roads and highways in pronghorn country, but the areas listed here allow public access to pronghorn habitat. Remember that wild animals are unpredictable and can be dangerous if approached. The best way to view wildlife is from a respectful—and safe—distance.

BUFFALO GAP NATIONAL GRASSLANDS IN SOUTH DAKOTA

These grasslands offer nearly 600,000 acres (243,000 h) of open prairie mingled with sections of rugged badlands. Buffalo Gap is home to many pronghorns, and most areas have roads or trails for sightseers.

HART MOUNTAIN NATIONAL ANTELOPE REFUGE IN OREGON

This unique refuge features an isolated, desert-like section of land that is home to some 2,000 pronghorns. Although they are spread throughout the refuge, most of the pronghorns tend to stay to the south and east of Lookout Point, in the flatter part of the refuge.

LITTLE MISSOURI NATIONAL GRASSLANDS IN NORTH DAKOTA

This vast region, located in western North Dakota, includes the Theodore Roosevelt National Park. Spread across Little Missouri's rolling prairie and badlands is an abundance of wildlife, including pronghorns. The western part of the grasslands area generally offers the best opportunities to see pronghorns.

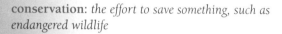

conservation: *the effort to save something, such as endangered wildlife*

evolved: *developed over a long period of time*

harem: *a group of females that all mate with the same male*

hemoglobin: *a substance in blood that helps carry oxygen to muscles*

predators: *animals that kill other animals for food*

sagebrush: *small, bitter-tasting shrubs found in the western United States*

tendons: *cords of tough tissue that connect muscles with bones or other muscles*